RASHALL JOYNER

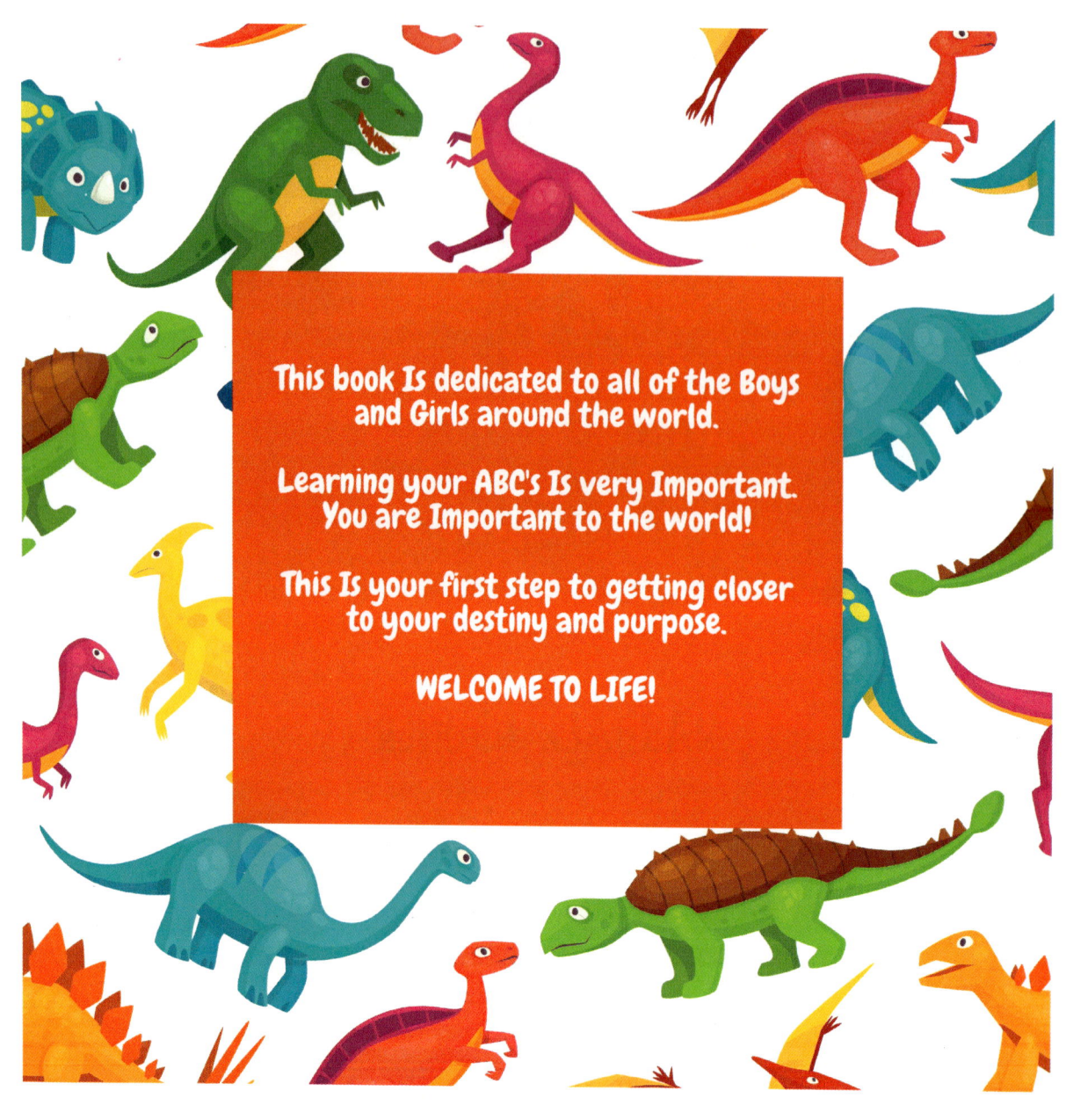

This book Is dedicated to all of the Boys and Girls around the world.

Learning your ABC's Is very Important. You are Important to the world!

This Is your first step to getting closer to your destiny and purpose.

WELCOME TO LIFE!

Aa

A

APPLE

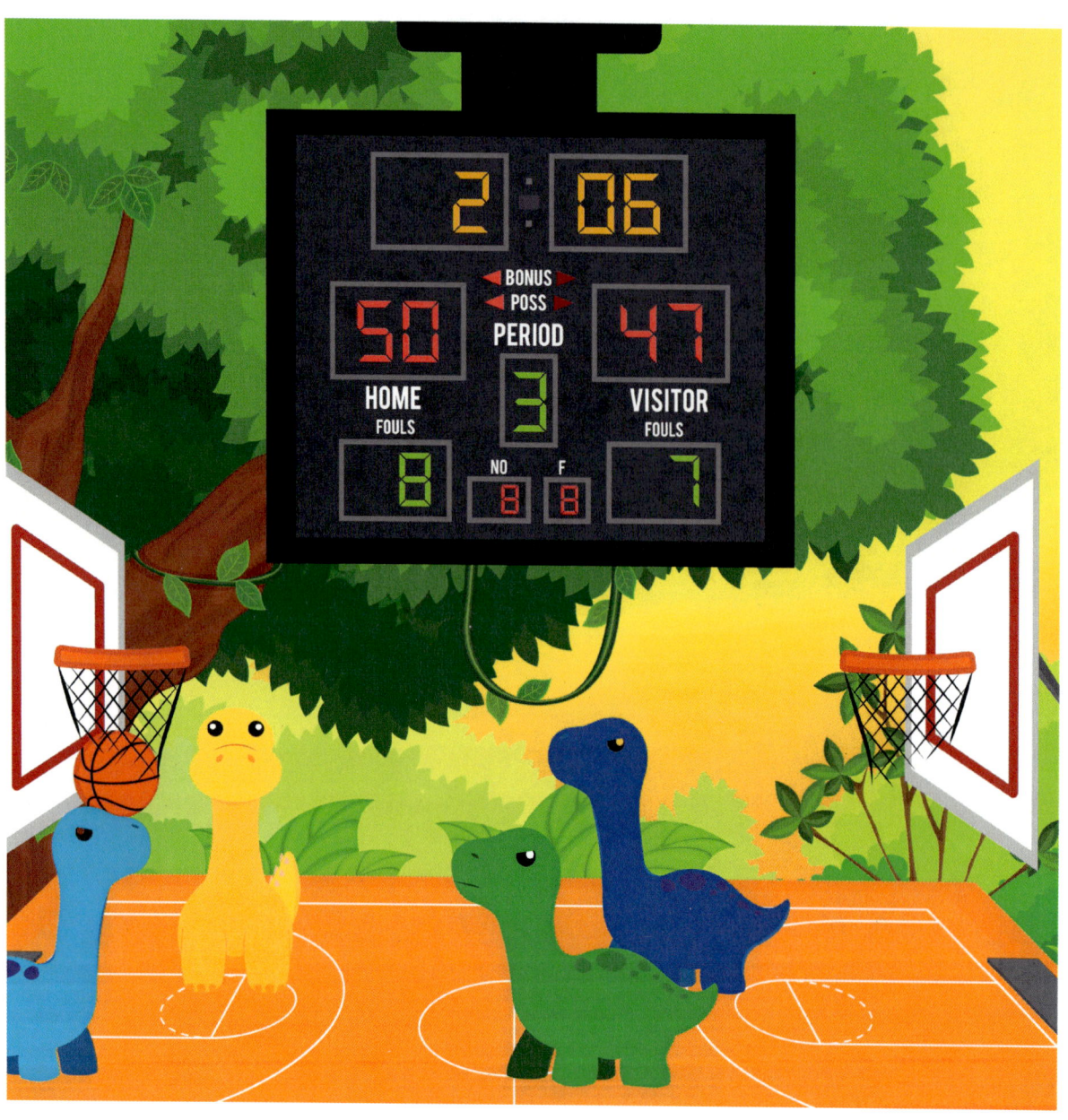

B

BALL

Cc

C

CAT

Dd

D

DOG

Ee

E

ELEPHANT

F

FROG

Ff

G g

G

GIRL

Hh

H

HELICOPTER

Ii

I

IGUANA

J

JACKET

Jj

M

Mm

MONKEY

Nn

N

NIGHT

Oo

O

OCTOPUS

Pp

P

PIRATE

R

RAT

Ss

S

SUN

Uu

U

UMBRELLA

Vv

V

VIDEO GAME

Ww

WATERMELON

Yy

Y

YO-YO

Zz

Z

ZEBRA

Made in the USA
Middletown, DE
14 May 2022